Original title:
Coconut Grove Serenity

Copyright © 2025 Creative Arts Management OÜ
All rights reserved.

Author: Dexter Sullivan
ISBN HARDBACK: 978-1-80581-555-6
ISBN PAPERBACK: 978-1-80581-082-7
ISBN EBOOK: 978-1-80581-555-6

Nature's Calm Embrace

In the shade, the monkeys swing,
Their antics make the palm trees sing.
A toucan flaunts its beak so bright,
As crabs dance with comedic delight.

Sun-kissed laughter fills the air,
While flip-flops fly without a care.
A hammock sways, with joyful creaks,
As sloths stare on with lazy beats.

Secrets of the Tropical Hideaway

Beneath the leaves, a secret spy,
A gecko winks with a watchful eye.
The breeze whispers jokes to the piper's tune,
While lizards plot under the watchful moon.

Coconuts fall with a thud and a roll,
Testing the prowess of every soul.
With flips and flops, beach games ensue,
A sandcastle crumbles, and laughter breaks through.

Gentle Breezes and Forgotten Shores

On the shore, a crab tells a tale,
Of a fish lost his shoes, oh what a fail!
The waves chuckle, a mild delight,
As seagulls squawk out their silly plight.

A shell plays music, a conch-sorcerer,
While fronds dance along, the prancer's merry blur.
A sunburned tourist with a comical cheer,
Spills his drink and lets out a cheer!

A Quiet Retreat in Nature's Arms

In nature's lap, the turtles ponder,
While a squirrel feasts with dreams of wonder.
A breeze brings whispers of sunburned tales,
And a parrot yells, "Watch out for the snails!"

As wildlife chuckles, the palm trees sway,
With fruit falling down in the silliest way.
Finding peace in this comical spree,
Life's quirks nestled together, full of glee.

Balmy Nights and Oceanic Dreams

Under the stars, the coconuts sway,
Crabs doing salsa on the sandy ballet.
Laughter spills out with the ocean's roar,
As seagulls critique our dance on the shore.

Mangoes are laughing, ripe on the vine,
While palm fronds whisper, 'Life's just divine.'
Moonlight plays tricks on our flip-flop race,
As shadows join in, giving chase to our grace.

Echoes of a Past Paradise

Shells clatter together like old friends' chat,
Fish flip with a grin, in this watery vat.
The beach towel lies, a canvas of fun,
As sunblock wars wage under the midday sun.

Crabs boasting tales of the ocean's great might,
While we nap and dream through the shimmering light.
One silly seagull tries to steal our fries,
With a goofy strut and the cheekiest eyes.

Nature's Canvas at Dusk

The sunset drips hues like a painter in awe,
While beachgoers stumble, with cool drinks to draw.
A dolphin pops up with a splashy surprise,
Soon followed by giggles under blush-tinted skies.

Flip-flops forgotten, it's a game of tag,
As biting mosquitoes begin to brag.
We dance on the sand, with a silly charade,
Under stars that twinkle, in cosmic parade.

Elysium of the Beachside Retreat

In this slice of heaven, the cocktails flow free,
As sandy toes wiggle, in sheer jubilee.
A parrot swoops down with a joke in its beak,
While we burst out laughing, no need to speak.

The sun dips below, a fabulous glow,
And flip-flops fly off in the twilight show.
We toast to the breeze, and to laughs that we share,
In this paradise spot, free from worry and care.

Moments Caught in Tranquility

In the shade where palm trees sway,
I found a crab trying to play.
He danced like he forgot his rhyme,
And I chuckled, savoring time.

A parrot squawked a tune so loud,
It tried to impress a sleepy crowd.
I laughed so hard, I lost my drink,
But who needs juice when you can think?

Gentle Waves, Gentle Souls

The sea rolled in with a belly flop,
While seagulls laughed, they just can't stop.
A dolphin winked, a cheeky tease,
I swear it giggled with the breeze.

As children splashed with gleeful yells,
A sunburned dad in a wave fell.
His sunglasses flew like a frisbee,
And we roared with laughter, all so dizzy.

A Harbor for the Weary Mind

On a rock, a tortoise sat,
Wearing shades—imagine that!
He pondered life, or so it seemed,
While beachgoers laughed, all sunbeamed.

A fisherman fished with quite a flair,
His hook tangled in his hair!
With every cast, he made a scene,
And we cheered him on, quite mean.

Luminous Pathways in the Sand

Footprints led to a jellyfish's sting,
A child declared, "It's a sticky thing!"
The mom just sighed, "Oh dear, beware!"
As laughter bubbled in the salty air.

We built a castle, crowns on our heads,
The tide rolled in, took all our beds.
We shrieked in fun, splashed not a care,
While our sand kings vanished, lost in the air.

The Heartbeat of an Island Calm

In the shade where palm trees sway,
A crab tried to dance, but lost his way.
With coconuts tossed like a game of catch,
Mangroves giggled, as if they'd hatch.

The lizards ran races on a narrow beam,
Chasing sunsets, in a blissful dream.
Even the waves wore a playful grin,
Tickling the toes as they crashed in.

A toucan laughed at its own loud screech,
While the sun poked fun, like a wise old beach.
Here every whisper holds a lighthearted feel,
As if even nature's spinning a wheel.

So join the party of shadows and sun,
In this quirky paradise, where laughter's the fun!
With palm fronds swaying in a jubilant dance,
Come dip your toes, take a chance!

Petals of Peace on the Sea Breeze

A floating leaf laughed at a passing boat,
Waving hello with a silly note.
The ocean chuckled as it played at tease,
While jellyfish bobbed with the greatest of ease.

Butterflies stumbled in the sunshine glow,
Chasing a breeze that wouldn't let go.
With flowers sprinkled on the sandy flat,
Dancing around like a giggling cat.

Seagulls squawked, what a honking delight,
While the crabs shared secrets under the night.
The wind carried tales of tomfoolery,
In a place where fun is the only decree.

As petals swirl in the gentle embrace,
Nature's a jester in this boundless grace.
Come laugh with the tides, let your worries cease,
Among blooms and breezes, find your peace!

Coastal Reveries in Sunlit Corners

Shells worn and weary tell a quirky tale,
Of sandcastles built in a bright, sunny gale.
A crab in a hat, played the role of a king,
Where all were invited, laughter took wing.

Seashells clinked like glasses at a feast,
While fish wore tuxedos, their charm never ceased.
A starfish danced, but forgot its groove,
With waves as the music, they all tried to move.

Seagulls took turns wearing cool sunglasses,
While the beach had its share of funny gasses.
Each wave would roll in, with giggles so loud,
As if the ocean itself was proud.

So in this corner where joy radiates,
Come crack a joke with the tide as it waits.
With sun beaming down on a whimsical sight,
Laughter is key, bring it into the light!

An Interlude of Nature's Bounty

A squirrel with style pranced along the shore,
While the breeze played tricks, asking for more.
Bananas waved, trying to join the fun,
With grapes 'round their necks, like they're on the run.

The waves kept time with a comedic beat,
As seashells clapped beneath tiny feet.
A dolphin popped up, gave a silly grin,
Knowing full well, even it couldn't swim!

Coconuts rolled down the sandy hill,
Like marbles in play, with agility and skill.
A parrot told jokes while perched on a log,
Making the sunbeam laugh like a fog.

Amidst nature's bounty, joy takes center stage,
Where fun-quenching smiles are all the rage.
So come, take a seat, let the antics unfold,
In this lively theater where stories are told!

Bliss Beneath the Starlit Sky

The crabs dance while the moon shines bright,
They clink their shells, what a silly sight!
A parrot jokes, perched on a tree,
"Is it me or is the ocean quite free?"

Fishes swim by, with a wink and a grin,
Waving their fins as if to begin,
A conch shell laughs, 'What's the fuss?'
"We've got the waves, no need to rush!"

Secrets of the Coral Coast

In a hammock, a cat dreams of fish,
While a dog plays fetch with a foolish wish.
The sea whispers secrets, like a playful tease,
"Life's a beach, come join with ease!"

The sun dips low, painting skies in pink,
While a tiny crab finds a treasure to blink.
A turtle chuckles, 'I'm slow but I'm wise,'
As he waves goodbye, with a spark in his eyes.

Dancers of the Evening Light

Fireflies twirl in a disco of glee,
While lizards groove on a branch of a tree.
The breeze gives a wiggle, a shimmy, a sway,
"Come dance, my friends, till the break of day!"

In the shadows, a frog plays the lute,
While a parakeet sings, with a touch of a flute.
The stars join the fun, twinkling with cheer,
"I don't know the moves, but we all can persevere!"

Embracing the Island's Heart

A pineapple wears a jaunty old hat,
While coconuts giggle, just look where they're at!
Laughter erupts from the waves on the shore,
"Come join our party, who could want more?"

The palm trees sway like they're in a ballet,
With coconuts chuckling, "This is our day!"
Bananas join in, with a slapstick affair,
"Who knew the jungle could throw such a fair?"

Embrace of Nature's Embrace

In the shade where palm leaves sway,
Monkeys plot their cheeky play.
Coconuts drop with a thud,
The sandman smiles at the sudden flood.

Seagulls squawk their daily news,
While tourists wear mismatched shoes.
A crab boogies on the shore,
Declaring dance is never a bore.

Laughter bubbles like the sea,
As sunburned folks shout, "Look at me!"
Life's a fairway of joyful glee,
Underneath this sunlit spree.

Here, nature laughs in shades of green,
Where even the lizards bask and preen.
In this embrace, the day grows bright,
With quirks that make the heart take flight.

Solitary Sands and Silhouettes

A shadow struts on golden sands,
Trying hard to get a tan—but stands!
Flip-flops flying with every step,
While onlookers giggle, not inept.

The sunflowers sway, just out of reach,
While clowns juggle seashells on the beach.
A lone beach ball rolls astray,
As clueless surfers surf away.

Turtle hatched to boundless space,
Waddles off to find some grace.
In a world of crabs and thrills,
This silly saga gives us chills.

With each wave, a chuckle blends,
Nature teaches, laughter never ends.
In silhouettes, we find our track,
Life's a jest, just sit back!

Lullabies of the Tide

Waves croon softly, a rhythmic hum,
As sleepy dolphins start to strum.
Seashells whisper secrets deep,
While crabs dance on in their snappy leap.

Out on boats, the tourists drift,
With fishing rods and dreams to lift.
"Did I catch a fish?" they cry,
Oh no, it's just a passing pie!

A gentle breeze teases the air,
While beach bums lounge without a care.
Seagulls cackle at their plight,
As laughter swells with the coming night.

The tide sings songs of joy and cheer,
With every wave that washes near.
So close your eyes, let laughter glide,
These lullabies will be your guide.

Interlude Among the Trees

Beneath the canopy, shadows play,
Where squirrels chase their nuts all day.
Lemons drop from branches high,
While nearby bees hum and fly.

A vine twists round a laughing trunk,
While wise old owls snooze, all funk.
Hikers tripped on roots adorned,
In nature's jest, they are reborn.

Birds create a concert loud,
As humans gather, feeling proud.
A ruckus here, a giggle there,
Among the trees, we shed all care.

In this interlude, wild and free,
Let the laughter flow like trees.
Nature's charm, sweet and vast,
With every chuckle, hold it fast.

Serenity Beneath the Canopy

Under palms, a squirrel giggles,
Peeking at the beach from the thickets.
A crab, in its odd little dance,
Moonlights the sand with its sideways prance.

Sunlight filters through big leaves,
A parrot jests, while we believe,
That every sip of coconut drink,
Could cause us all to start to think.

A chubby tourist on a swing,
Twirls 'round like a big, funny thing.
He'll call it grace, we'll see the show,
As a coconut plops—THWACK!—on his toe.

In this paradise, laughter unfurls,
With wind that whispers and twirls,
The vibe is silly, the world bright,
Under this canopy, all feels just right.

Reflections on Aquamarine Waters

Beneath the waves, a fish sings low,
In a top hat, it steals the show.
While turtles float with a fussy grace,
Trying hard not to lose their face.

A beach ball bounced from cheek to cheek,
It lands on a lifeguard—what a sneak!
Water splashes, and giggles ensue,
As he fumbles the ball in his rescue.

Paddleboarders in their frantic glide,
Look like they're surfing on butter, slide!
Each splash brings on a chorus of shouts,
"Is it me, or the ocean, that's got the clouts?"

Reflections shimmer with a glint of fun,
As the sun sets, we all come undone.
With ice cream smeared on our happy face,
These waters hide a wacky embrace.

Breaths of the Island Wind

A breeze rolls through, a gust of jest,
In skirts of grass, it plays its best.
Whispers secrets to the naïve
Like, "This weather's here to make us leave!"

A flamingo stands, oh-so-absurd,
Trying to balance, it looks disturbed.
As wind blows hats from heads so proud,
Shouts of surprise mix with the crowd.

Tropical scents filled with a joke,
Coconut shells, what a fun bloke!
Charged with echoes of laughter's bliss,
As island folk share a comical kiss.

Here, the air's a giggle machine,
Tickling stories in spaces between.
With every puff, a chuckle spins,
As time unwinds and the laughter begins.

The Sound of Waves Embracing Shore

Waves leap up in laughter's spree,
Splash at the feet of a dancing bee.
Feet in the sand, a jester bows,
To the rhythm of time, under the boughs.

A seagull steals a popped corn treat,
With a squawk that makes folks back off their seat.
Each flap of its wings sends the kiddos squealing,
A comedy show that needs no concealing.

Shells sing like pots in a cooking band,
Creating tunes all over the sand.
"Clap your hands!" call the sea to the flat,
While a crab joins in, just like that.

With every crash the ocean greets,
The shore giggles in quirky beats.
Together they dance in sand and surf,
The laugh of the waves, our island's turf.

Nature's Serenity Unfolded

In a hammock swaying free,
Laughter blends with rustling leaves.
Sipping coconuts on spree,
Nature's joke, the heart believes.

Monkeys swing with careful grace,
While parrots squawk, a loud surprise.
A crab waves, joins the race,
As if saying, 'Look, no disguise!'

Barefoot dreams upon soft sand,
Tickling toes with sea's delight.
Seagulls dance in daytime's band,
Invisibility at height!

But lo, the sun begins to drop,
The shadows play in sly relief.
We chuckle, wishing it won't stop,
The joy of nature, oh, so brief!

Journey to the Island's Core

Set sail on a boat of dreams,
With a crew of giggling friends.
Steering towards the golden beams,
Whispers of fun that never ends.

Coconuts in hats we wear,
Pirate jokes that fill the air.
A treasure map, or maybe snack?
Finding goodies, we won't lack!

Sailing forth with glee and zest,
Every wave a goofy dance.
The sea's a stage, we're all jest,
Life's a show, we take a chance.

At last, we land on sandy shores,
With footprints forming silly lines.
As seagulls watch our playful roars,
We swear it's bliss in these designs!

Tropical Whispers of the Heart

Among the trees, a secret hum,
The whispers laugh, oh what a sight!
Each fruit a riddle, ripe and plumb,
The mango shakes its juicy might.

A gecko grins, in shade it lurks,
While crickets chirp a dance-off tune.
We giggle at their tiny quirks,
As butterflies take flight at noon.

The breeze carries tales of yore,
Telling jokes of nights gone by.
With every wave that hits the shore,
We laugh at clouds wafting high.

Nature's humor fills the air,
A playful jest in every view.
We raise a toast to life, we share,
In tropic bliss, we start anew!

Moonlight Over Palm Fronds

When moonbeams tickle palm tree tops,
The night unfolds a playful grin.
With shadows dancing, laughter hops,
We dive into the fun within.

A crab in shades tries to lounge,
As starfish spread their twinkly toes.
The beach is full of laughter's sound,
While owls hoot their gossip prose.

Dreams are tangled in the breeze,
As fireflies join the cheering crew.
Each pop and flash is sure to tease,
As night unveils its silly view.

With moonlight as our guiding spark,
We host a party, wild and free.
In this enchanted, crazy park,
We're all just kids, lost at sea!

Tropical Whispers

In a land where coconuts sway,
Monkeys plot their mischief play.
Sipping drinks with little umbrellas,
Laughter echoes, oh what fella!

A parrot mimics every word,
While tourists' antics seem absurd.
Flip-flops flopping, sandals fly,
Hats blown off as seagulls cry.

Lush Oasis Dreams

Swaying palms in twilight's glow,
A chubby crab moves too slow.
Beach balls bouncing, kids will shout,
"Hey, catch this!" with joyful doubt!

Sandcastles rise, but quickly fall,
As waves come crashing, heed the call.
Parents giggle, kids will squeal,
In this fun, we all can feel.

Beneath the Palm Canopy

Underneath the swaying leaves,
A sleepy iguana weaves.
Sunbathers snooze, some hardly pale,
While nearby, a sand crab tells a tale.

A kite gets stuck, a child in tears,
As laughter bursts, dispelling fears.
Flip-flops tangled in a race,
Lively antics fill this place.

Serenity of the Shoreline

Waves that whisper, tickle toes,
While children chase the ebb and flows.
A sun-kissed dog digs in the sand,
Wagging tails, oh isn't life grand?

An ice cream truck jingles near,
As flavors swirl, we all cheer.
The sunset drapes in hues so bright,
While goofy dances bring pure delight.

Serenity Found in the Rustle of Leaves

Swaying palms dance, oh what a sight,
Their whispers tickle, bring pure delight.
A coconut drops, bonk on my head,
Laughing at nature, she's playful instead.

Sipping a drink with a tiny straw,
While crabs sneak up, just to get their paw.
The sun winks at clouds, plays peek-a-boo,
Nature's own jesters, always so true.

Tropical breeze, a tickle and tease,
The rustle of leaves puts me at ease.
Watch out for the birds, with mischief in flight,
They'll steal your sandwich, oh what a sight!

A hammock sways gently, calls out my name,
In this leafy theater, life's just a game.
Belly laughs echo, they bounce off the trees,
Here in the grove, I'm as light as the breeze.

The Promise of an Island Dawn

Morning breaks with a coffee in hand,
The smell of pancakes drifts through the sand.
Seagulls are arguing, what's new today?
While cheeky monkeys join in the fray.

Sunrise paints skies in colors so wild,
Nature's canvas is delicately styled.
Laughter erupts as the waves start to play,
Fish splash around, it's their version of ballet.

A beach ball rolls down, what a sweet chase,
Running after it, I trip on my face.
The crabs are all chuckling, shells clattering loud,
While I try to blend in, concealed by a cloud.

With each rising sun, there's mischief anew,
Island mornings, what a whimsical view.
Embracing the chaos, with giggles and cheer,
In this sweet paradise, nothing to fear.

Journeys Through the Emerald Green

Across emerald fields where laughter resides,
I stumble on vines, oh what a ride!
With flip-flops slapping and spirits so high,
A frog croaks a tune, as I hop on by.

The path leads to wonders, both funny and odd,
Where turtles are racing, it's truly a nod.
They waddle and wiggle, not caring a bit,
As I cheer them on, giving it my wit.

A toucan flies in, with a flair for the show,
Calls out with a honk, "Come join in the flow!"
Peeking through bushes, see what's out there,
A band of iguanas who just don't care!

With every step taken, there's joy to be found,
In this playful forest, where silliness abound.
A journey of giggles, a dance with the green,
In the heart of the grove, pure happiness seen.

Whispers of the Tropical Twilight

Under the stars, where the breezes tease,
Fireflies flicker, like tiny bright keys.
Chairs creak and groan, they join in the fun,
While I sip my drink, watching day come undone.

A lizard steps out, with a swagger so bold,
In his little world, he's a sight to behold.
Beneath the moonlight, the crickets recite,
A symphony strange, what a whimsical night!

Tiki torches dance, casting shadows around,
As laughter and stories like waves, they abound.
Flipping through moments, we giggle and sigh,
Time's just a trickster, oh my, oh my!

Embraced by the warmth of the night's gentle sway,
The grove calls my name, inviting to stay.
With whispers of joy and a sprinkle of glee,
I find my delight in this tropical spree.

The Calm Between the Waves

In a hammock hung so low,
I'm swaying with a gentle flow,
A crab sings tunes of ancient lore,
While I snack on chips, who could ask for more?

Seagulls laugh as they steal my fries,
While I pretend to close my eyes,
The tide rolls in with a cheerful shout,
As flip-flops squish, that's what it's about!

Palm trees sway with a playful grin,
Their fronds tickle my head like a win,
The ocean whispers jokes so bold,
I chuckle softly, feeling old!

With every wave that dances near,
I sip my drink and let out a cheer,
For in this bliss and sunny haze,
I'll dance with life, for days and days.

Lullabies of the Island Breeze

The breeze hums softly through the leaves,
While I giggle at what mischief weaves,
A squirrel darting, a coconut falls,
As I catch the laughter that nature calls.

Children play, their laughter bright,
Like fireflies winking in the night,
The sand tickles toes, a sweet delight,
While a sandcastle upholds its might.

Coconuts rolling down the way,
Make me wonder if they wish to play,
The breeze teases, the waves adore,
And all my worries I might ignore.

Under the sun, our shadows prance,
To the rhythm of this lazy dance,
In paradise, fun is the theme,
With dreams that flutter — yes, how they beam!

Shadows of the Sunset

As day bids farewell with a big bright smile,
The sun dips low, but it's still worth the while,
Shadows stretch out, a comical sight,
I become a giant – what a delight!

The horizon blushes in shades of gold,
While stories of fish and sailors unfold,
A dog chases crabs, oh what a show,
Wagging his tail, he's a pro, don't you know?

As the sky turns into a patchwork quilt,
A joke from the waves makes my heart wilt,
"Catch me a sunset!" the clouds seem to tease,
While I giggle and flop like a gentle breeze.

With laughter echoing into the night,
I wear the moon's glow — a playful light,
In this colorful dance of day and night,
Every shadow whispers, "What a delight!"

Swaying Palms and Silent Dreams

The palms sway gently as if they know,
The secrets of laughter and sunshine's glow,
I dream of tacos, of fish in the sea,
And a hammock wrapped just around me.

Stars peek out from the curtain of dusk,
Whispers of night bring a sweetened musk,
The sound of the waves, a soft lullaby,
I drift into dreams while the crickets sigh.

The moon's a comedian, shimmering bright,
Joking with me in the still of the night,
With tickles from clouds that sail across,
I laugh at the stars, oh what a toss!

The island knows how to share a grin,
With every moment, I'm caught in a spin,
So here's to the dreams that drift and sway,
In the arms of laughter, come what may!

Reflections on Still Waters

A coconut swayed in the breeze,
With a grin, it danced with ease.
The tide tickled its shiny skin,
It chuckled softly, a silly grin.

Crabs in tuxedos strut with pride,
While fish wear shades on a water slide.
They splash around, the laughter flows,
In this place where the fun never slows.

Palm trees gossip, swaying high,
About the gulls who think they fly.
A sunburnt tourist laughs so loud,
As he trips on waves, feeling proud.

In this paradise, life is a game,
Where sandcastles rise and fall the same.
With every wave that crashes near,
The humor brews in sunshine cheer.

Echoes of the Island

Seagulls argue over a stray fry,
While monkeys leap from tree to sky.
A breeze carries the scent of fun,
Laughter mingles with rays of sun.

The old boat bobbing at the shore,
Complains about each wave's uproar.
While surfers chase the ocean's zoom,
Tugging their boards like they own the room.

Sandy toes and ice cream cones,
Sing a song of beachy tones.
As sunburned folks dance out of time,
Each move a step, each step a rhyme.

Island life, a playful jig,
With mermaids giggling, oh so big.
Beneath the stars, they share their tales,
As crickets chime with happy wails.

Midnight Revelations by the Sea

Under the moon, the waves jest loud,
A turtle wears a party shroud.
The shells conspire in a quiet plot,
To prank the sailors who snooze a lot.

The fishing nets lay out a song,
Where anglers stumble, all night long.
With lanterns shining bright as day,
They boast of fish that got away.

Mysterious shadows dance on sand,
While friendly crabs take a stand.
In midnight revels, the secrets spill,
As laughter rises with every thrill.

The nightingale plays a tune off-key,
While palm trees wave, oh can't you see?
In this whimsical, starry embrace,
The silly antics create endless space.

Harmonies of the Dusk Sky

As the sun dips, a parrot squawks,
Her gossip floats on sandy walks.
With fish flip-flopping, tales unfold,
In hues of pink and hints of gold.

Chasing stars in a coconut bowl,
The night reveals each playful soul.
A crab recites his poetic feast,\nWhile all the gulls applaud, at least.

A hammock sways with dreams so bright,
Where sleepyheads cuddle tight at night.
Life here is a carnival ride,
Where laughter rolls like the evening tide.

Beneath the sky's harmonious glow,
Friends toast the waves with a hearty hello.
Each bubble of joy, a secret shared,
In the silly serenade, none are spared.

Rhythm of the Gentle Waves

The waves are dancing, what a sight,
They giggle and splash, oh what delight!
A crab in a top hat waltzes by,
While seagulls squawk a karaoke lullaby.

The surfboards line up for a race,
But flippers and fins join the chase.
An octopus plays the ukulele,
As dolphins cheer in their own ballet.

Sandy toes tap to the ocean's beat,
Though seagulls swipe snacks to cause a retreat.
Children build castles, they're towering high,
Until a rogue wave says, "Oh my, oh my!"

A beach ball bounces, boisterous fun,
Till it lands on a sunbather's bun.
So much laughter on this sunny shore,
Where every wave whispers, "Come back for more!"

Hidden Sunlit Refuge

In a nook where the palm trees sway,
A squirrel's having a dance party today.
He's wearing sunglasses, looking so cool,
While the crickets cheer him on in the pool.

A hammock swings, with a cat in a hat,
Pretending to nap, but being quite fat.
The sun drips honey on this lazy scene,
As lazy bumblebees hum with glee in between.

A turtle attempts to join the fun,
But trips on a leaf—it's a real pun run!
With every tumble, there's laughter galore,
As they picnic and giggle on this forested floor.

Beneath the shade, the chatter flies,
While ants perform plays, oh what a surprise!
Nature's laughter, a joyful refrain,
In this hidden spot, no worries remain.

Breeze Through the Fronds

The breeze strolls in with a silly grin,
Tickling the leaves, making them spin.
Parrots gossip about the day,
While a lizard strikes poses, come what may.

Coconuts roll like balls in a game,
And every drop leaves a giggling fame.
A playful gust tries to steal a hat,
But it's just a ruse, oh what of that!

Tropical fruits dangle, ripe and bright,
While monkeys swing in sheer delight.
They steal a snack, then dash away,
In this playful jungle, there's no gray.

The shadows dance with a lively jig,
While frogs make music, oh so big.
The symphony of fun fills the fronds,
In a world where laughter truly responds.

Tranquil Retreat in Paradise

In a calm spot where the sun meets the sand,
A walrus sunbathes, feeling quite grand.
While nearby, a moody crab plays dead,
"I'm just resting!" it squeaks—oh, what a spread!

With a drink in hand, floats the dreamiest chair,
A flamingo joins in, showing off flair.
They sip from coconuts, pink umbrellas so bright,
While fish join a conga, creating a sight!

The laughter of children fills the warm air,
As a goat in a sweater staunchly declares,
"This is my spot!" with a wink and a grin,
Turning sunbathing into a competitive win!

In this harmonious nook, worries all fade,
While the humor of nature dances, unmade.
A place where serenity meets playful cheer,
In this tranquil retreat, let's all hold dear.

The Rhythm of Tides and Time

The ocean waves dance and play,
Tickling toes in the sunny spray.
Seagulls squawk with silly glee,
Stealing fries, as bold as can be.

Time drips slow like melting ice,
While crabs scuttle, oh so precise.
Shells and laughter litter the shore,
Who knew beach days could be such a chore?

Sunburnt noses and goofy hats,
Build sandcastles with goofy chats.
Waves crash down, a watery dance,
Who needs a plan? Let's leave it to chance!

Flip-flops flying, a comical sight,
Running for cover from bites of the night.
In this frolic, all worries unwind,
Life's too funny, let's not be confined!

Daydreams in the Shade of Palms

Under the palms where shadows play,
I nap with a snack, just dreaming away.
A squirrel steals my sandwich, oh what a tease,
I laugh and I chase, with crumbs in the breeze.

Daydreams drift on a lazy cloud,
While I'm lost in thoughts, never feeling proud.
The sun tickles my nose, just like a tease,
I'll trade this for nap time, if you please!

Lizards sunbathe, a comical crew,
While I sip my drink, it's almost too blue.
They blink in surprise as I toss them a crumb,
The palm fronds sway, while I break into hum.

In this shade, the world feels bright,
With laughter and snacks, all in sight.
Let time stand still, let the fun flow free,
In this drowsy paradise, just you and me!

Celestial Nights in Island Skies

Stars twinkle above like jokes on a string,
As crickets chirp, they start to sing.
Moonlight giggles on the waves, so spry,
Even the dolphins leap up high!

Fireflies twirl like choreographed dreams,
While we roast marshmallows, plotting our schemes.
I drop a skewer, it sizzles and sparks,
As laughter erupts, we light up the dark.

Tales of the day swirl in funny tones,
Under the blanket of stars and soft moans.
Each wave whispers laughter, secrets untold,
In this cosmic comedy, we feel so bold.

Time floats by on a breeze of delight,
As we dance with shadows in the moonlight.
With giggles and joy, we cherish the night,
In this playful paradise, everything feels right!

Breezes Soft as Whispered Secrets

Gentle breezes tease the palm fronds,
As I chase kites like playful wands.
Surprise! A seagull swoops down low,
Plucking my hat — oh, where'd it go?

The market buzzes with laughter and cheer,
As vendors shout jokes for all to hear.
Yet I stumble on bananas, oh what a sight,
Falling with grace, now isn't that right?

Laughter floats with the fragrant air,
As children launch water balloons with flair.
I dodge and weave, but oh, what a mess,
Drenched in glee, not a moment to stress!

Soft as whispers, the breezes retreat,
With the sun setting low, it's time for a treat.
Let's revel in fun, let our hearts take flight,
In this quirky paradise, everything feels right!

Tranquil Shores: A Coastal Reverie

Seagulls squawk like gossip queens,
Chasing crabs in sunny scenes.
The waves giggle as they crash,
Suggesting we should make a splash.

Palm trees sway with lazy grace,
They seem to dance in a slow race.
Sunbathers play peek-a-boo,
As waves keep saying, "I see you!"

Children build castles tall and grand,
While sandsticks cling like an eager hand.
A dog decides to dig a hole,
Claiming this beach as its very own goal.

Sunsets paint the sky so bright,
Whispering jokes of day to night.
With laughter and the ocean's tune,
We find our joy below the moon.

Embrace of the Ocean's Edge

Sandy toes and sticky treats,
Funny hats in summer heats.
A beach ball bounces, what a sight,
It flies away—oh, what a flight!

Surfboards wobble, oh so fun,
Falling off is just begun.
Splashing water flies up high,
Like a birthday cake—oh my!

Tide pools giggle, waves clap hands,
Tickling toes with soft commands.
Fish pretend they're in a play,
In this comedic watery ballet.

Even the sun can't help but grin,
As everyone joins in the din.
We dance with laughter, side by side,
In this embrace where joy can't hide.

Lush Echoes Under a Starry Canopy

Butterflies flit, acting shy,
While crickets chirp their lullaby.
A monkey hangs by its tail,
In a vine dance, it won't fail.

Stars winks like they know a joke,
As night wraps us in a cloak.
Fireflies blink, a disco ball,
Inviting us to dance, we fall!

The moon chuckles in delight,
As shadows play in soft moonlight.
Laughter echoes in the trees,
Feeling festive in the breeze.

Bamboo rustles like it sings,
As if it knows the joy it brings.
In laughter's arms, we sway so free,
Under this vast celestial spree.

A Dance of Light and Sea

Sunshine bounces on the tide,
Little fish begin to glide.
With a flip and a splash, they tease,
Just look at all those giddy seas!

Sailboats bob like party hats,
While dolphins play, doing splats.
We wave and cheer from the beach,
As they leap like they're out of reach.

When clouds moan, we all just grin,
Waiting for the rain to begin.
Umbrellas pop like flowers bloom,
Laughter chases away the gloom.

With each wave that rolls on in,
The playful spirit makes us grin.
Under the sun's warm, golden plea,
We find our joy beside the sea.

Echoes of Peace Beneath the Stars

The crabs are dancing in the moonlight's glow,
Their pinching antics steal the starry show.
A lilo floats by, wearing a silly hat,
While seagulls gossip, 'Did you see that?'

Waves tickle toes, with whispers of the night,
Shells are giggling, oh what a delight!
Jellyfish bounce like they've lost their way,
While the stars chuckle and join the play.

Sandcastles crumble, their reign now done,
The tide takes over, but oh, what fun!
A beach ball bounces, breaking the calm,
It flies past the palm, a joyful psalm.

Beneath the stars, there's laughter so grand,
A breeze tickles cheeks, warm as a hand.
The night twirls on, in a humorous twist,
Under the sky, not a worry exists.

Calming Currents of the Tropics

The banana boat swings, as the kids take a ride,
With splashes of laughter, it's a wild, fun tide!
The parrots squawking, "Time for a treat!"
As dolphins leap high, in a playful beat.

A hammock is swaying, held up by a dream,
While others are trying to catch a cold cream.
The sun laughs brightly, with a wink in its eye,
"Don't fret about sunburn, just give it a try!"

Footprints in sand tell stories of joy,
Of sandcastle battles, girl against boy.
The tide rolls in, whispering sweet songs,
While everybody joins in, it never feels wrong.

A coconut falls with a thud and a clatter,
"Is this breakfast or just cosmic chatter?"
With smiles all around, it's a tropical tease,
As the warm breezes blow, bringing us ease.

Leafy Secrets of Hidden Shores

Beneath the palm fronds, a secret unfolds,
A chattering squirrel, with stories retold.
The lizards debate, 'Who runs the best race?'
While crickets compose, in their leafy space.

The coconuts giggle, with each little fall,
"Who'll take a hit? Come on, not at all!"
A turtle strolls by, wearing bright shades,
Saying, "Life's a beach, in these leafy glades."

The breeze curls around, like a playful friend,
Tickling the leaves, as they twist and bend.
A squirrel with acorns, can't find the stash,
"Where did I put them? Oh! What a clash!"

Amongst the shadows, laughter takes wing,
With echoes of joy that the forest can bring.
Each rustle a giggle, each breeze a cheer,
In leafy confidences, we hold so dear.

A Serenade to the Setting Sun

The sun waves goodbye, with a wink and a grin,
As the day gets sleepy, and the night creeps in.
Fish flopping around, in their splashy ballet,
While crabs start a chorus, "Join us today!"

With flip-flops forgotten, feet dance in the sand,
As shadows grow long, they take a stand.
The twilight performs, in colors that spark,
Balloons in the distance make the sky feel like art.

Guitars strum sweetly, under the sky's hue,
While fireflies join, with their soft, twinkling crew.
The night takes a bow, the stars shine so bright,
In this joyful serenade, everything feels right.

So dance to the rhythm, of the waves and the breeze,
With laughter echoing, like waves through the trees.
As the sun slips away, it leaves us with fun,
In the heart of the tropics, where joy's never done.

Stillness in the Flora

In the shade of leaves so bright,
A squirrel takes a nap, what a sight!
The flowers giggle, gossiping low,
While ants march by in a tidy row.

Breezes tease the palm trees tall,
They sway and dance, as if at a ball.
A lazy lizard lounges with grace,
In this tranquil, silly space.

The butterflies join in the fun,
Chasing each other under the sun.
With petals and pranks, they leap and flutter,
Oh, the joy, it makes my heart stutter!

So here I sit, laughing at life,
With nature's antics, no room for strife.
The stillness hums a joyful tune,
Under the antics of the playful afternoon.

Under the Watchful Moon

The moon peeks in to have a glance,
As shadows grab the stars for a dance.
Crickets chirp a comedic tune,
While raccoons plot to steal the spoons.

A wise old owl shakes his head,
"Keep your secrets, don't be misled!"
The fireflies flicker, giggles abound,
Creating rhythms in the night's sound.

The waves crash softly, a laugh or two,
As silly seabirds tumble through.
The ocean humors the night's parade,
Under the moon, worries do fade.

With each gentle breeze, a smile's born,
Nature's jesters at the breaking dawn.
So let the night's joy unfold with glee,
In the watchful glow, we're all carefree.

Warmth of the Coastal Kisses

The sun rolls up like a big, round pie,
As gulls swoop down, oh my, oh my!
Beach towels flutter as flip-flops run,
In this playground where everyone's fun.

The waves chase shells, laughing with glee,
While sandcastles bow to the sea.
Seagulls squawk, plotting a heist,
For a chip or two, oh, they're quite nice!

Kids make wishes on boogie boards,
Mom's sunscreen tactics, A+ rewards.
With laughter echoing, joy in the air,
Every salted breeze makes you unaware!

As night rolls in, the grill's aglow,
With stories and laughter, fun's on show.
Under the warmth of coastal kisses,
We welcome the night, embracing our wishes.

Dreams on the Ocean's Edge

Sandy toes and sun-kissed cheeks,
Pirates of laughter, that's the technique!
The horizon winks and folds its arms,
While jellyfish dance, casting their charms.

A crabbing contest just turned wild,
With hermit shells and a giggling child.
The ocean whispers silly rhymes,
Smoothing out all our silly crimes.

Castaway dreams on a raft of fun,
While seagulls play games, no need to run.
The tide brings tales of whimsy and cheer,
In line with the surf, there's nothing to fear.

So let your spirit ride the waves,
In this ocean laughter, we are brave.
As sun dips low, the day's nearly done,
With dreams afloat, we've had our fun.

Enveloping Loved Ones in Nature's Peace

In the shade where coconuts hang low,
Laughter echoes where the breezes blow.
Feet in the sand, giggles arise,
As crabs play tag under sunny skies.

With a coconut hat on my dear friend,
A fashion choice I cannot commend.
They clap their hands, I burst with glee,
Next week, we'll launch a crab jubilee!

Sipping drinks topped with tiny umbrellas,
I toast to my friends, my cool fellow-dwellers.
We dance with vigor, feet all a-shuffle,
In a coconut-themed raucous kerfuffle!

As the sun dips low behind palm trees,
We crack jokes like shells in the salty breeze.
Life's coconut, served with a slice of fun,
We're enveloped in peace till the day is done.

Sanctuaries of Solitude by the Shore

Waves giggle softly as they kiss the sand,
A lonely coconut jokes on a landstand.
With toes in the tide, I ponder and muse,
Wondering why I chose these crazy shoes.

Seagulls squawk in their comedic tone,
Diving for snacks that I can't condone.
I laugh as they squabble and tumble around,
Creating a laughter that's ocean-bound.

A picnic laid out with snacks galore,
I try to eat but I'm sandy for sure.
Sandwiches sprinkled with the finest grit,
I take a bite and I secretly quit.

In the twilight hush, solitude calls,
But it's hard to resist those gregarious squalls.
Even alone, I still find delight,
In the antics of nature, a comical sight!

Harmonies Found in Nature's Embrace

Beneath a palm, we find our chats,
While pesky raccoons plan their spats.
With coconuts rolling, ideas do flow,
We argue who's best at a hula-hoop show.

The sun paints our cheeks a bright merry hue,
As birds carry melodies of mirth anew.
Nature's orchestra plays snickers and chuckles,
While I chase my hat, oh, how it buckles!

Friends share secrets like seashells on the shore,
Each one a treasure, we can't help but adore.
We take goofy selfies, all smiles and grins,
Nature's our backdrop; here, laughter wins!

Together we bask in this harmonious cheer,
Where humor is loyal, and joy's always near.
In this natural embrace, it's plain to see,
Life's a wild concert, come sway wild and free!

Embracing the Stillness of Twilight

As day bows out with a wink and a grin,
We gather around, let the night fun begin.
Twilight whispers secrets, stars start to peek,
With a coconut lantern, I play hide and seek.

The moon giggles softly, nudging the sun,
While shadows dance, oh what silly fun!
I trip on my feet, land right on my face,
But my friends find my fumble a charming embrace.

With marshmallows roasting on sticks held high,
Even the birds laugh, I can't deny.
In this peaceful moment, laughter fills the air,
As we hiccup bright giggles without a care.

The night wraps us gently, like a cozy old quilt,
We revel in joy; we've had quite the spilt.
Embracing stillness, we treasure this thrill,
For in twilight's laughter, we find our goodwill.

Play of Light on Water

Sunlight dances on the lake,
Splashing ripples like a cake.
Fish jump high to steal the show,
While I just sit, the jokes will flow.

A seagull lands with quite the flair,
Trying to steal my picnic fare.
He squawks a tune, so out of tune,
I laugh aloud beneath the moon.

Breezes tease my floppy hat,
With every gust, I lose my spat.
Laughter echoes all around,
As I chase my hat on the ground.

The sun waves bye at the end of day,
While water's shimmering dance won't stay.
Tomorrow's jokes await the dawn,
In this paradise, my cares are gone.

Moments in the Mangroves

In the mangroves, shadows play,
Where crabs dance as if to say,
"Come join us, friend, it's all a game!"
Their sideways moves, a silly fame.

A heron stands with regal grace,
Till a wave sends him from his place.
He flaps and squawks, a comic show,
While I, in stitches, watch him go.

The mangrove roots reach out like hands,
As if to guide us through the lands.
I trip and tumble, laugh out loud,
While nature smiles, a leafy crowd.

Sunset spills gold on the scene,
The mangroves twist in hues so keen.
Life here is a wondrous jest,
In every moment, I'm truly blessed.

Floating on a Tropical Daydream

A hammock swings like a gentle ride,
In dreams I float, nowhere to hide.
With coconuts, I start a race,
But they just roll, oh, what a chase!

The sun's a glow worm in the skies,
As I sip juice and close my eyes.
A parrot squawks with its own flair,
Its fashion sense, too wild to bear!

I spot a dolphin doing flips,
It's clearly working on its scripts.
As I chuckle with pure delight,
I swear it winked with all its might!

In daydream's realm, the laughter flows,
As time drifts by, and no one knows.
A breeze whispers secrets to the trees,
In this float, I'm lost with ease.

Enchanted Pathways in the Breeze

The pathways twist like a silly worm,
Where every turn brings a new term.
The wind giggles through the leaves,
Where mischief brews and nature weaves.

While I tread lightly on the ground,
I hear a squirrel make a sound.
It chats away, like it's a pro,
In its own world where giggles grow.

Laughter trails behind my steps,
As butterflies perform their reps.
A lizard darts with comic speed,
In this enchanted place, I'm freed.

With every breeze, a chuckle stirs,
In this realm where magic purrs.
Games of joy await ahead,
As smiles bloom with every tread.

Beneath the Fronds

Under palm leaves, squirrels play,
Chasing shadows, sunbeams sway.
A coconut drops with a goofy thud,
As laughter echoes, mixed with mud.

Seagulls squawk, and crabs parade,
With tiny hats, they're unafraid.
The breeze tickles in a playful way,
While tourists giggle at their hay-day.

Flip-flops flop; it's quite the scene,
A dog trots by, but he's not keen.
He's after ice cream meant for me,
With funny faces, oh so free.

The sun dips low, it's time for fun,
Silly dances, everyone!
Beneath the fronds, we take a spin,
Where laughter lives, and joy begins.

Peace Awaits

In lazy hammocks, dreams entwine,
As bugs buzz, and sun-rays shine.
A cheeky monkey drops a shell,
And leaves us laughing, all is well.

Flip-flops squeak like a weird old tune,
Crickets chirp beneath the moon.
The world slows down, just take a seat,
With snacks of mango, life's a treat.

Waves crash softly, whispering dreams,
While jellyfish dance in shimmering streams.
Here's to the smiles, to the silly life,
Where laughter cuts through all the strife.

Under stars, we share a toast,
To the quirks of nature, we love the most.
Each sunset sparks a glowing cheer,
In this warmth, peace lingers near.

Silent Poetry of the Tide

The ocean whispers with bubbly prose,
As fish swim by in fancy clothes.
Tiny tides giggle, swirl, and sway,
Chasing shells in a froggy ballet.

A crab pulls faces, striking a pose,
While dolphins splash, in stylish throes.
The sand tickles toes, that's quite a surprise,
Under the sun that winks and sighs.

On the shore, a sandcastle stands,
With flags of seashells, kingly hands.
It leans a bit, the tide's in charge,
As laughter crashes, we all enlarge.

The sun sinks low, the sky ignites,
As silhouettes dance in the fading lights.
This silent poetry, a joyful tide,
Where hearts feel free and laughter's our guide.

A Tapestry of Sunset Colors

The sky bursts in shades of jelly bean,
Orange, pink, and a touch of green.
As kids giggle, painting the sand,
With wild strokes that are truly grand.

Seagulls prance like they own the place,
Stealing snacks with a charming grace.
They squawk in delight, plan their next trick,
As we giggle, it's quite the pick.

The surf rolls in, a bubbly crew,
Holding seashells like they are new.
With sand in our toes, we jump and shout,
This funny scene, there's no doubt about.

With colors fading, it's time for dream,
Under stars, we all gather and beam.
This tapestry glows, a whimsical sight,
Where laughter lingers through the night.

Resting on the Coastal Hush

Upon the shore, where silence plays,
We lounge and share the sun's warm rays.
A pelican's dive makes us all cheer,
As waves giggle, so crystal clear.

A sun hat flies, caught on a breeze,
Chasing laughter through palm tree leaves.
With sandwiches squished, and drinks all around,
We toast to silliness that's always found.

The sunset glimmers, a quirky waltz,
As a crab strolls by, it's no big fault.
In the twilight glow, we stretch and sigh,
As breezes carry our thoughts up high.

With sleepy eyes and happy hearts,
We gather memories, each one imparts.
In coastal hush, we pause the day,
Where joy resides, in a quirky way.

Embracing Nature's Gentle Call

In the shade where breezes play,
A squirrel steals the show today.
He wears a nutty little grin,
While birds join in, in feathered din.

Sunshine dances on the leaves,
While I plot what mischief weaves.
The lizards laugh, their tails on fire,
As I chase after dreams, inspired.

Coconuts roll with giggles, too,
One bumps my head, oh what a view!
The palms sway like they're in a trance,
And I can't help but join their dance.

Later, I sip a drink so sweet,
While crabs attempt a silly feat.
I cheer them on with a loud shout,
As nature's chaos swirls about.

Luminescent Silhouettes at Dusk

As dusk descends in twilight hues,
The shadows stretch in funny shoes.
I trip over, the sand's a prank,
While fireflies glow, a glowing flank.

The stars appear, much like my dreams,
They twinkle bright in silly beams.
A heron swoops, it's quite a sight,
While I shout, 'Oh! Stay out of flight!'

Palm trees sway with a wobbly cheer,
As I declare, 'I live in here!'
The moon winks in mischievous glee,
While waves curl up, just to tease me.

Laughter echoes in the breeze,
Nature's joke brings me to my knees.
I'll dance under these starry veils,
Where humor flows in gentle trails.

A Soliloquy Under the Palms

Under the palms, I talk to the air,
The coconuts chuckle, 'We're quite a pair!'
A crab drags by, a sly little chap,
He winks at me, it's quite a tap.

The breeze whispers secrets, all too bold,
While I relay tales of daydreams told.
The waves applaud my humble speech,
With foam-topped licks, they're within reach.

The sun dips low, a merry affair,
As the shadows mime in playful flair.
I laugh along, it's such a thrill,
Nature's comedy, give me more still!

A parrot squawks, I've lost the plot,
But in this ruckus, I've found my spot.
Under the palms, life feels like play,
With every moment, I'm whisked away.

Enchanted Moments by the Shore

By the shore, the waves concoct glee,
With every splash, there's joy for free.
I build a castle, it leans and bends,
As the tide giggles, it wobbles and ends.

Seagulls swoop, in feathered beams,
They steal my fries, or so it seems.
With laughter bubbling in the air,
I toss them crumbs, I hardly care.

The sun dips low, it's quite a jest,
Painting the sky in hues that rest.
A dolphin leaps, a friendly tease,
While I sip coconut with such ease.

Moments like these, forever fresh,
In laughter and chaos, we are enmeshed.
Life's little winks, as the day turns warm,
A dance of joy in nature's charm.

www.ingramcontent.com/pod-product-compliance
Lightning Source LLC
Chambersburg PA
CBHW050317100526
44585CB00016BA/1548